Jack the

This slim volume came about as a result of the extensive research I carried out in preparation for my forthcoming book *The Inevitable Jack the Ripper,* which is due for publication at the end of August, 130 years after the first 'Canonical' murder attributed to the psychotic serial killer known as Jack the Ripper.

What follows is a series of images, some modern, some from the 1880s or thereabouts, which I feel tells an awful story and provides an important primer to *The Inevitable Jack the Ripper.*

Many thanks to all those who have helped me on this journey – a culmination of a decade of interest, fascination, travel and research.

- Paul Christian

The imposing statue of Lord Salisbury, the then-Prime Minister, guarding the entrance to Hatfield House, in Hertfordshire.

Jack the Ripper-era head of the Metropolitan Police, Commissioner Sir Charles Warren. A former British Army officer, archaeologist of the Temple Mount in Jerusalem and the man who ordered the infamous 'Goulston Street Graffito' to be washed off.

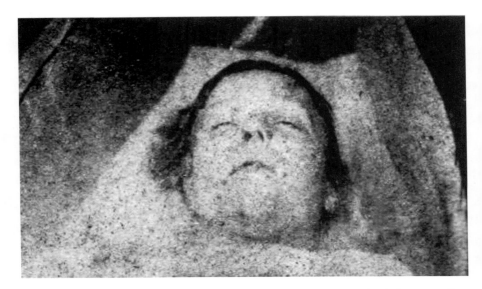

Polly/Mary Ann Nichols was the first of the so-called 'Canonical' victims of Jack the Ripper. She was found dead in the early hours of August 31, 1888. Her throat had been slit twice, from left to right and her abdomen was mutilated with a jagged wound. There were several other incisions across her abdomen. In common with all the other 'Canonical' victims, Nichols was a prostitute.

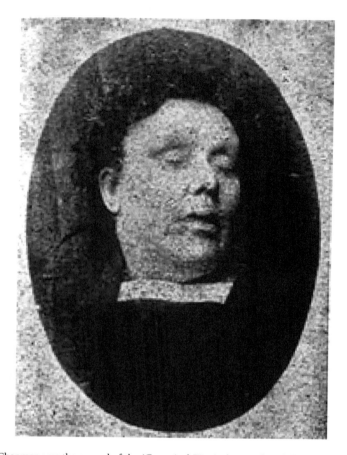

Annie Chapman was the second of the 'Canonical Five', she was found dead in a yard at 29 Hanbury Street, Spitalfields, at around 6am on September 8, 1888.
In a sickening escalation from the first murder, her throat had been cut from left to right and she was disembowelled. Her intestines had been thrown over her shoulders and part of her uterus was missing.

Elizabeth Stride, known as 'Long Liz', a native Swede, was found dead in Berner Street (now Henriques Street), in Whitechapel, on September 30, 1888. Her throat had been cut, but aside from an abrasion, there were no other wounds. Stride was the first of the so-called 'Double Event' killings and it has been suggested her killer was disturbed prior to being able to satisfy his depraved urges. Indeed, mere hours later and around 15 minutes' walk away, another woman lay dead and the results were awful.

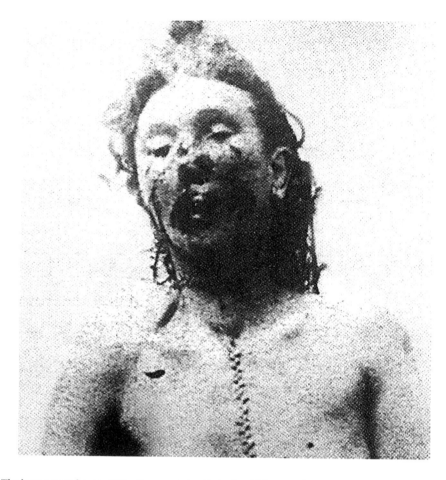

The horror meted out to Mitre Square victim Catherine Eddowes, who was found horribly mutilated in the early hours of September 30, 1888, was perhaps the most savage of all the 'Ripper' killings aside from that inflicted on Mary Kelly. The severity could have been a result of the lack of satisfaction brought about by killing 'Long Liz' Stride around an hour earlier and not being able to mutilate her body.

Her face was cut with arrows carved into her cheeks, her throat was cut, her kidney was removed and she was disembowelled.

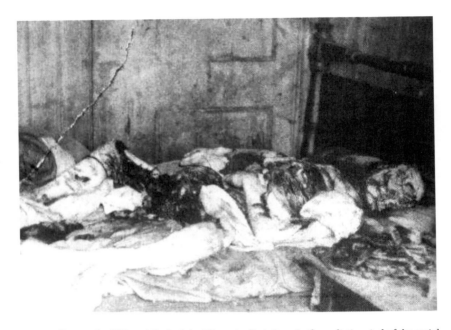

Mary Kelly was the fifth and final of the 'Canonical' victims. In the sadistic mind of the serial killer, her killing could be considered his 'masterpiece'. It was the most savage of all the Whitechapel Murders, which themselves set a new standard for brutality. She was the youngest of the 'Canonical' victims, at just 25, and was originally from Ireland.
Her body was torn apart on November 9, 1888.
Being inside a secluded room in Miller's Court, Dorset Street, Spitalfields, the killer had time to act out his horrific fantasies after Kelly was dead.
Her abdomen was sliced open and all her viscera was removed and littered around the room, her breasts were cut off, along with her face and her thighs were partially hacked through to the bone, with some of the muscles taken out.

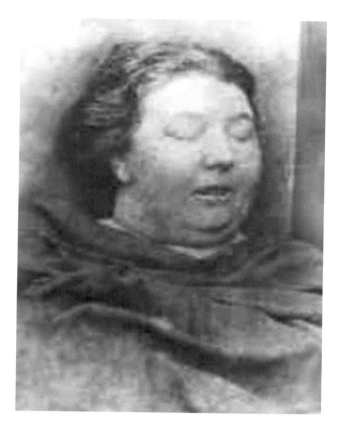

A potential early Jack the Ripper victim, Martha Tabram was stabbed 39 times in a crazed attack on August 7, 1888 in George Yard. Some believe she was murdered by the Ripper before his usual modus operandi was established and her death presented the work of a serial killer in the making.

Hanbury Street, where Annie Chapman was found dead in 1888, is now at the bustling heart of London's East End, packed full of curry houses and other eateries, bars, pubs and trendy pop-ups. While a bit rough around the edges, it is a far cry from the impoverished area where Chapman was slain 130 years ago.

Henriques Street, in Whitechapel, which was formerly known as Berner Street, where Elizabeth Stride was found with her throat cut in 1888. It was the first location of the infamous 'Double Event' in which the Ripper is believed to have killed twice in one night a short distance apart.

Mitre Square, in the City of London, was the scene of one of the Ripper's most savage killings, that of Catherine Eddowes. Being in the City of London also meant that it brought another police force into the investigation, which had until that point been the preserve of the Metropolitan Police. Today Mitre Square is in the shadow of St Mary Axe, colloquially known as The Gherkin.

Miller's Court, in lawless and deadly Dorset Street, where Mary Kelly was so brutally killed and mutilated. The site no longer exists and is now an industrial unit.

Pinchin Street, in East London, where the 'Pinchin Street Torso' was found in September 1889. The discovery is now seen as part of the Thames Torso Murders, a lesser-known serial killing spree before, after and at the same time as the Jack the Ripper murders. At the time the Torso murders were linked, not only by the rabid downmarket press, but by police who added the killings to their Whitechapel Murders files. A woman's headless and legless torso was discovered in a railway arch by PC William Pennett. It was believed the torso was dumped where it was found after being dismembered elsewhere.

Once this site at Victoria Embankment was the under-construction police headquarters of the then-Scotland Yard. Dismembered remains of a woman were found close to this spot in 1888 and, like the Pinchin Street Torso, the 'Whitehall Mystery' as this discovery became known, was part of the Thames Torso Murders. It was linked both contemporarily, and in some cases afterwards, to the Jack the Ripper/Whitechapel Murders.

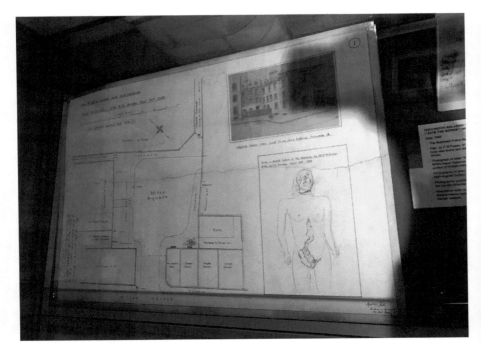

Police and coroner artefacts at the Royal London Hospital Museum, in Whitechapel, detailing the murder of Catherine Eddowes in Mitre Square. Another display case a short distance from this, in the same museum, features a replica of the skeleton of the infamous 'Elephant Man' Joseph Merrick, a Ripper-contemporary and curiosity for credulous and mawkish Victorians.

Microfilm of *The Herts Advertiser* newspaper from November 10, 1888 which reports the murder of Mary Kelly. The St Albans-based newspaper is still in existence today. The author worked for its sister title the *Welwyn Hatfield Times*.

St Patrick's Catholic Cemetery, in Leyton, East London, where the final 'Canonical' Jack the Ripper victim, Mary Kelly, is buried.

The grave of Mary Kelly. The inscription reads: "None but the lonely hearts can know my sadness. Love lives forever."

Victorian murderer Severin Klosowski, who poisoned women he was romantically involved with. Some believe he was Jack the Ripper, despite his markedly different modus operandi.

Leavesden Asylum Cemetery, in Hertfordshire. Local rumour wrongly holds that Jack the Ripper is buried here. The site does have a strong Ripper link, however, as it is where Aaron Kosminski, an inmate, died before being buried at a Jewish cemetery, in East London, in 1919. Kosminski is now a popular Ripper suspect and was committed to the asylum, after a spell at Colney Hatch – another asylum, where he was sent in 1891 just three years after the last 'Canonical' Jack the Ripper murder.

The author's rough sketch of Aaron Kosminski.

Artist Walter Sickert (photographed in 1911) a strong Ripper suspect. His links to the murders and involvement in the murky art scene at the time of killings is explored in *The Inevitable Jack the Ripper*.

The grave of Victorian artist and satirical cartoonist Starr Wood, in Rickmansworth, Hertfordshire. Wood was wrongly suspected of being Jack the Ripper and chased by an angry mob at the height of 'Rippermania'. He escaped by hiding in a railway station. The pursuit of Wood highlights the febrile atmosphere at the time of the killings, which was exacerbated by a failing police force and lurid press coverage.

A modern-day 'Ripper Walk' in Mitre Square. There are a number of money-spinning historical walks focusing on the crimes attributed to Jack the Ripper, where tourists and history buffs are guided to the crime scenes and other important sites in East London.

The author at the microfilm reader in St Albans Library. The resource is invaluable in accessing contemporary accounts of the murders, which have helped to establish context, new theories and basic facts in the case. They are a wonderful tool for researchers.

Printed in the USA
CPSIA information can be obtained
at www.ICGtesting.com
LVHW061345161123
763944LV00044B/17